11,532

789

Eeckhoudt, Jean Pierre Vanden, 1919-
    A butterfly is born.   N.Y., Sterling, [1973]
94p.   illus.   (Sterling nature series)

1.Butterflies.   I.Title.

A

BUTTERFLY

IS BORN

STERLING NATURE SERIES

A
BUTTERFLY
IS
BORN

Text and photographs
by J. P. Vanden Eeckhoudt

STERLING
PUBLISHING CO., INC. NEW YORK
Oak Tree Press Co., Ltd.
London & Sydney

STERLING NATURE SERIES

Eighth Printing, 1973

Sterling Publishing Co., Inc.
419 Park Avenue South, New York, N.Y. 10016
British edition published by Oak Tree Press Co., Ltd., Nassau, Bahamas
Distributed in Australia and New Zealand by Oak Tree Press Co., Ltd.,
P.O. Box 34, Brickfield Hill, Sydney 2000, N.S.W.
Distributed in the United Kingdom and elsewhere in the British Commonwealth
by Ward Lock Ltd., 116 Baker Street, London W 1
Manufactured in the United States of America
ISBN 0–8069–3506 –5   UK 7061 2282 8
3507 –3

CONTENTS

BUTTERFLIES AND MOTHS

Of all insects, butterflies and moths are certainly the most attractive. Their forms and colors are rich and varied beyond description. The very word "butterfly" makes us think of summer, of sunny days and of flowering meadows.

The fields, the woods, the hills, the mountain crags all have their particular species. The butterflies of spring are followed by those of summer, and they in turn are followed by the butterflies of autumn. There are some, too, which appear only in winter.

There are some which live for several months; others survive for only a few weeks; others again for only a day or two. Most of them do not fly far, but some are travelers and migrate across the oceans.

Some fly in daylight and become drowsy as soon as the sun disappears; others wake up only in the twilight; and many do not leave their hiding places until it is quite dark.

Camberwell Beauty
(magnified 2 times)

1.   (magnified 4 times)

Illus. 1. The CHALK-HILL BLUE is a small butterfly, very common in summer. The specimen shown here
is spreading its four silvery-blue wings in the sun. The
antennae, or feelers, with their delicate rings of black
and white, are spread wide in front of the head.

2.   (magnified 3 times)

Illus. 2. The wings of the small PEARL-BORDERED FRITILLARY butterfly are reddish-brown with black markings. Its antennae have the club-shaped tips which distinguish the butterfly from the moth. The small black objects on the sides of the head are the eyes. Between the antennae are the two hairy palps or feelers.

Dry hillsides open to the air and the sun, the flower-decked slopes of mountains, and sunny banks by the roadside are the favorite places of the Fritillaries. They skim over the ground, gliding with wings fully extended, and alight on flowers of thyme or thistle to sip the nectar or to warm themselves in the sun.

The Fritillary shown in Illus. 3 has fallen asleep for the night on a thistle. Its wings are raised and folded together above its back — the sleeping position of all butterflies, as distinct from moths. The photograph shows the features mentioned on the previous pages.

Here we can also see four legs — thin, jointed and angular. All insects have six legs, but in some, like this one, the two front legs are shrunken from lack of use and are hidden by the body. The undersides of the wings have a graceful pattern in yellow, brown and black.

3.
Fritillary
(magnified 4 times)

A moth has many features which distinguish it from a butterfly. Its shape is less graceful, its body is thicker, it has a heavy coat of down. The antennae, fringed or feathery, never have the clubbed end of the butterfly's. When a moth is at rest its wings fold over each other to cover its body.

We can see these features in the NUN MOTH, more commonly called BLACK ARCHES, shown in Illus. 4. It is spending the day asleep on the leaves of a wild cherry tree. Its white wings with their pattern of black are folded down over its body, almost completely concealing it. The wide feathery antennae are extended sideways. This moth is found in late summer in gardens and orchards.

4.
Nun Moth
(magnified 5 times)

The life of butterflies and moths is calm and carefree. They have no fierce competition, no brutal appetites and no scenes of violence. Like the GEOMETER (Illus. 5), they unfold their wings, take to the air, sip nectar, lay their eggs and die.

But their whole life cycle is not spent in the air. Moths and butterflies are merely the final stage in a long series of transformations. The cycle, leading from the lowly, greedy caterpillar to the butterfly, will be shown in the following pages. The SMALL TORTOISE-SHELL, a common European butterfly, will serve as an example of this transformation. The whole extraordinary story will be shown as it was recorded and photographed in natural conditions, stage by stage, from the egg to the perfect insect. Then some examples of other kinds of butterflies and moths will give an idea of the many variations which Nature plays on this theme.

5.
Geometer
(magnified 6 times)

6. Small Tortoise-Shell   (magnified 2 times)

THE SMALL TORTOISE-SHELL

During the first warm days of spring four different insects come forth from their winter slumber or hibernation. They are the large Bumblebee in its coat of black, yellow and white; the Ladybug; the Brimstone Butterfly and the Small Tortoise-Shell.

The butterfly in Illus. 6 is a Small Tortoise-Shell. Its reddish wings, with their splashes of black and their edging of blue half-moons, are spread in the bright sunshine.

Born the summer before, this butterfly remains on the wing until the weather turns cold. Then it seeks shelter in a barn, an attic, a cellar or cave. Safe in its hiding place, it sleeps deeply for six or seven months. At last the light and warmth of spring rouse it. It likes to lie for hours at a time in some sheltered spot on the ground or on a flower, its wings spread wide, warming itself in the sun.

Sometimes another Small Tortoise-Shell joins it, and the two butterflies soar together in whirling flight. If they are of the same sex they part almost at once. If they are male and female they pair off. The eggs which the female has been carrying within her for several months can hatch if they are fertilized.

7.   (magnified 2 times)

Illus. 7. A pair of Small Tortoise-Shells have settled on a branch of pussy willow. (The butterfly at the top left-hand side of the photo is the female.) She is the only one actually on the branch and she will soon fly off. The male hangs motionless on the end of her abdomen, his wings closed and his legs and antennae folded against his body.

When the female's eggs have been fertilized, she spends several days fluttering about a patch of nettles— the only plant on which butterflies of this species will lay their eggs. She flies to and fro, closely circling the

8.　　　　　　　　　(magnified 1.8 times)

chosen clump, now landing on a leaf, now soaring rapidly away, but returning immediately. Soon she flies in smaller and smaller circles and at last she chooses a leaf near the top of a stalk. Clinging to the leaf, she bends back her abdomen and lays her eggs on the underside of the leaf (Illus. 8). When all the eggs are laid, the butterfly leaves them, never to return. She has a few more weeks of life, then dies like the rest of her kind. Until the late spring only the eggs and the larvae which emerge from them will remain to represent the species.

9.   (magnified 10 times)   10.   (magnified 40 times)

Illus. 9. The eggs—some 30 or 40 of them—are massed together on the underside of the nettle leaf. At the moment of laying, the eggs are covered with a gummy substance. When this dries they stick firmly together.

Illus. 10. Each egg is a tiny green pearl, 1/50 of an inch in diameter. The clear shell has nine narrow tooth-like ribs.

The eggs hatch three weeks after laying.

11. (magnified 10 times)

Illus. 11. Here we see two stages of the hatching. Some eggs are still whole. Through their shells (upper left-hand corner of the photograph) we can see a large black dot—the head of the tiny caterpillar within. Other eggs have nothing left but the empty shell, which resembles a cut-crystal goblet. These caterpillars have just hatched, and are now huddled together along a vein of the leaf (bottom right). Their community life has begun.

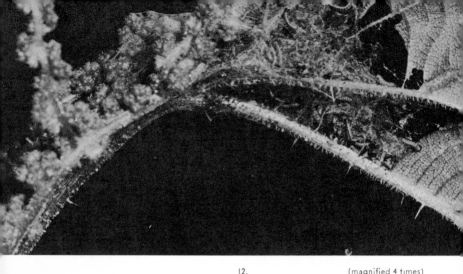

12.   (magnified 4 times)

As soon as the caterpillars are hatched, they begin to feed on the nettle. When they move, they leave behind them a delicate thread of silk, formed from a kind of saliva which jells when it is exposed to the air. Thus, their constant wanderings produce the tightly-packed network of lines in the center of the picture (Illus. 12). If a caterpillar happens to fall, it is saved by its thread.

After eating the leaf on which they were born, the caterpillars climb up to the top of the nettle plant, covering it with a silken shroud or tent (Illus. 13). Here they have a shelter and a platform on which they sun themselves from time to time. In a few days they devour all the leaves within their reach. Then they make their way down the plant in stages, weaving a fresh shroud

13. (magnified 2 times)

at each stop, and eat up the rest of the leaves. When one nettle has been destroyed in this way the caterpillars move on to another plant.

The caterpillars grow rapidly. Illus. 14 shows them at the age of about ten days. They have left their silken shelter and are nibbling on a nettle leaf, starting from the center and moving toward the edges.

Illus. 15 shows the caterpillars just under three weeks old. They are much larger, and the silk they spin is thicker. They no longer eat in such a systematic way.

The growth of caterpillars is interrupted from time to time. Because their skin does not stretch much, it rapidly becomes too tight for the growing insects. So the caterpillars must periodically leave their skin, as people give up clothes which no longer fit them, and emerge in a new skin, which all this time has been forming underneath the old one. The new skin allows room for further growth. When this in turn becomes too tight, it is cast aside in favor of a third, and so on.

The change of skin is called a moult. Illus. 16-23 show the main stages in a moult.

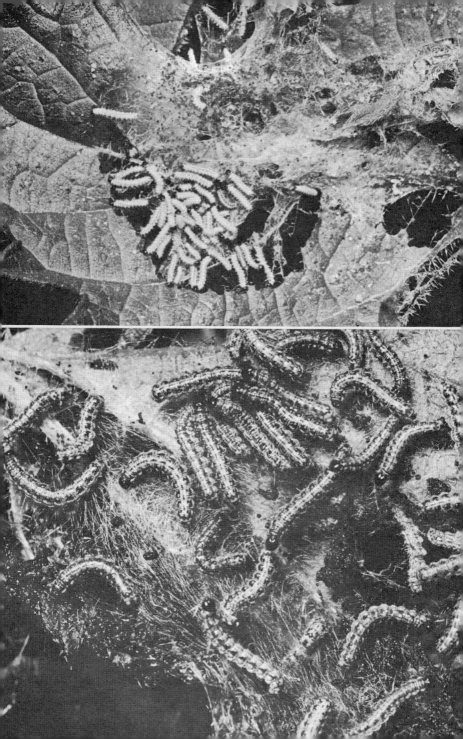

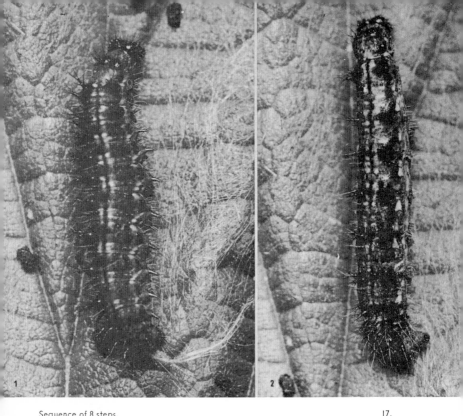

Sequence of 8 steps
(all magnified 6 times)

17.

Illus. 16. A caterpillar about to molt has taken up its station on a leaf. (Its head is toward the top of the photograph.) It has woven a little carpet of loose silk threads to provide support during the intricate movements of the molt. It then anchors itself to the framework of the silk with all its legs, becomes quite rigid, and remains motionless for two days.

Illus. 17. After this long pause the caterpillar returns to activity. While the old skin is held firmly in place by the network of silk thread, the caterpillar begins to wriggle forward in its new skin. The old skin seems to

18.

19.

slip down and back as it becomes more and more
strained behind the head.

Illus. 18. The caterpillar's efforts continue for several
hours. Its body swells, and suddenly the front part of
the old skin bursts open under the strain. The caterpillar emerges from the hole, clad in its new skin of
brilliant black and yellow.

Illus. 19. It frees the whole front of its body and
withdraws its head. The new skin is so large that it
forms creases.

20.   21.

Illus. 20 and 21. The caterpillar is almost completely free. It pulls itself out of the old skin, which remains fastened to the silk carpet.

Illus. 22. The caterpillar has just freed itself entirely. Its new skin is still damp and its hairs are sticking together in tufts.

The discarded skin has shriveled up. Only the horny skullcap which covered the head remains round. Com-

22. 23.

pare this shining black container with the caterpillar's head, which is still pale and soft. The head has grown a great deal in the short time since the molt.

Illus. 23. In a few hours the caterpillar is dry. Its prickly hairs stand up. Its head, a moment ago so pale and soft, hardens and darkens in the air. The caterpillar begins eating again, with an even greater appetite than before the molt. It grows more and more rapidly.

Sequence of 10 steps
Illus. 24-29 (magnified 3 times)

24.

The molt takes place four times in the course of the caterpillar's development. The photographs show a Small Tortoise-Shell caterpillar at the moment of birth and immediately before and after each of the four molts.

25.

Illus. 24.	Birth.
Illus. 25.	Before the first molt.
Illus. 26.	After the first molt.
Illus. 27.	Before the second molt.
Illus. 28.	After the second molt.
Illus. 29.	Before the third molt.
Illus. 30.	After the third molt.
Illus. 31.	Before the fourth molt.
Illus. 32.	After the fourth molt.
Illus. 33.	End of growth.

26.

27.

28.

29.

Illus. 30-33 (magnified 2.8 times)

While the old skin is being shed and the new skin is taking its place, the size of the caterpillar's body does not change. It is only the head that grows.

But during the period between two molts, the body of the caterpillar grows until it completely fits the skin and the skin cannot stretch any further. The time it takes for the caterpillar to become fully developed varies. Under favorable conditions, the caterpillar can become fully grown in five weeks.

30.

31.

32.

33.

Until the fourth molt the caterpillars live together, eating the same leaves, sheltering under the same silk tent, moving in a group from one nettle to another. By this time, there are far fewer caterpillars than there

35.   (magnified 3.5 times)

were originally, for birds, insects and disease have
killed many of them. Now, after the fourth molt, the
family breaks up. Each caterpillar goes off by itself
and makes a shelter in a nettle leaf which is rolled up
and held together by a few strands of silk (Illus. 34).
It leaves this shelter to eat and to spend long hours
stretched out on a leaf in the sun (Illus. 35). Its head
is at the left of the photo. The caterpillar is now very
handsome: velvety black with yellow dots and bands.
It bristles with stiff hairs and rows of spines. When
the caterpillar reaches a length of just over 1½ inches,
it stops growing.

36.   (magnified 3.5 times)

37.

A few more days pass. Then the caterpillar's mood
suddenly changes. Until now it has been greedy,
slow-moving and sluggish. All at once it becomes
nervous, restless and unsettled. It stops eating, and no
longer lies sunning itself. Instead it moves aimlessly
about on its nettle, and then climbs down and leaves
it forever. The caterpillar loses itself in the grass and
then reappears some distance away, crawling as fast
as it can along the bare earth of the path (Illus. 36).
It stops, hesitates and sets off again, growing more
and more restless all the time. It crawls up on a
number of different plants and at once crawls down
again. (In Illus. 37 the caterpillar is on the largest leaf
in the center.) It climbs onto the trunk of a poplar
tree, explores the bark in detail, and climbs down

again, still not satisfied. At last it disappears into a tangle of dead branches.

The next day, if we search carefully through the pile of wood, we find the caterpillar in the strange posture shown in Illus. 38. Fastened by its rear end to a sloping branch, it hangs down with its body curled in a semicircle. It has woven a pad of silk on the bark, and it clasps this with the hooks on its two legs at the rear of its abdomen.

In this position we can see the structure of the caterpillar clearly. The head is small and black. A series of grooves across the body divide it into twelve rings. Each of the three rings nearest the head (the thorax) has a pair of small black legs, hard and pointed. The nine other rings form the abdomen. Five of these have a pair of soft and flexible legs with wide soles for gripping surfaces. The small dots which run along the caterpillar's side are breathing holes, called stigmata.

Under the rather shaky shelter of its branch, the caterpillar remains motionless for several days, paying no heed to the sun or the wind, the dew or the evening chill. It has never taken such a long rest, not even before the molt. This time, too, the caterpillar is preparing to molt, but this molt will be of a different kind. The caterpillar is not only going to change its skin; it is going to change into a different kind of creature altogether. This stage (called a chrysalis) is a vital step in the metamorphosis or transformation which is to produce the butterfly.

38.   (magnified 4.5 times)

Illus. 39. The caterpillar at last emerges from its state of inactivity. It stretches and uncurls. Its whole body wiggles slowly. It expands and contracts for several hours. The caterpillar seems to be trying to crawl through the air.

Illus. 40. The skin becomes detached from the body and starts to slip downward. During this process the abdominal legs come off and the spines on the back

41.   42.

are separated. The caterpillar expands and contracts more and more rapidly until suddenly the skin splits behind the head.

Illus. 41 and 42. The creature that now emerges is soft and pale green, with rows of heavy spines. The squat and abruptly cut-off body is not at all like the hairy elongated body of the caterpillar.

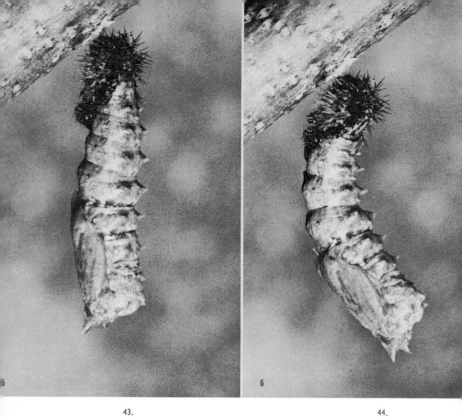

43.   44.

Illus. 43. The caterpillar's skin has been thrust off almost entirely. Now comes an extraordinary act of the chrysalis — removing the end of its body from the cast-off skin and fastening it to the silk pad on the bark.

Illus. 44. Arching its body sharply, it pulls the point of its abdomen — called the cremaster — clear of the skin. With a skillful twist, (Illus. 45), it fastens it

45.

46.

on the silk pad outside the skin. Now it has a firm grip and the chrysalis hangs motionless and rests (Illus. 46). Ten minutes have passed since it split the caterpillar's skin.

The chrysalis has lost the caterpillar's legs and rounded head, but now we can see the molds which in due time will produce the wings, the eyes and the antennae of the butterfly.

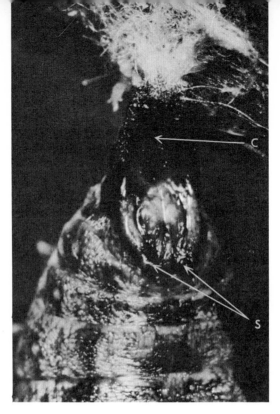

47. (magnified 12 times)

How does the chrysalis perform the acrobatic feat of freeing the end of its body from the old skin and fastening it directly to the silk, without falling off in the process?

Illus. 47. Throughout the maneuver, it holds onto the skin by the two dark projections (S) seen on the photograph, at the end of a horseshoe-shaped pad situated under the cremaster (C).

(The remains of the caterpillar's skin have been removed to expose the lower surface of the chrysalis.)

48.   (both photographs magnified 3 times)   49.

Illus. 48 is the same as Illus. 46: the chrysalis has just freed itself.

Illus. 49. This photograph was taken several hours later. The chrysalis has reached its final form. Its external skin has hardened and taken on a brown and gray color. (In some specimens the color may be paler, with flecks of gold.) We can see the twin horns on the head more clearly in this photograph. The caterpillar's skin dries up and becomes brittle; finally it falls off or is blown away by the wind.

June: two months have passed since the Small Tortoise-Shell laid its eggs on a nettle.

There is intense activity going on throughout the animal world. The starling is singing beside its nest in the tall cherry tree; blackbirds and hedge sparrows are rearing their broods in the shade of the bushy hedgerows. The peaceful countryside is alive with the friendly song of crickets. Bees and flies of all kinds murmur in the flower-strewn meadows.

Great numbers of butterflies appear when the weather is good. They flutter everywhere, sipping the nectar from flowers, sunning themselves on bushes, on tree trunks, on the ground. But no Small Tortoise-Shells are to be seen. Those that were out in the spring are dead, and the caterpillars (larvae) from their eggs have not yet completed their transformation. They are still in the chrysalis state. Beneath their hardened skin their organs are being completely remodeled, a process which takes at least two weeks. Then one last molt will release the perfect insect.

Sequence of 12 steps   51.   52.
(all magnified 2.5 times)

Illus. 51. During its long period of stillness the chrysalis has changed color. Its dull exterior has gradually become translucent so that we can almost see through it. It gives some inkling, here and there, of the coloring of the butterfly.

Illus. 52. At last, without warning, the covering of the chrysalis splits. The opening widens rapidly. A triangular panel begins to open at the urging of the insect within.

53.   54.

Illus. 53. The panel opens wider: a round black head appears.

Illus. 54. Suddenly two hairy elongated organs unfold and stretch out in front of the head. They are the butterfly's palps or feelers.

By fits and starts the insect emerges from its covering sheath.

55.

56.

Illus. 55. The butterfly pushes with all the strength of its legs against the exit panel. Inside, its clubbed antennae and long proboscis (nectar-sucking tube which projects from the butterfly's head) are securely encased.

Illus. 56. The antennae and proboscis withdrawn from their sheaths are now free. The wings are beginning to emerge from their cases. There has been a slight mishap: the butterfly has caught one of its antennae in one of the filaments or threads of its proboscis. The other filament is already curling up.

57.   58.

Illus. 57. Clutching the branch and twisting forward, the butterfly withdraws its abdomen from the chrysalis. The wings are free and hang down limply.

Illus. 58. The butterfly is born! Still weak and helpless, it clings to the empty sheath. In this position its wings hang down, still limp, thick and crumpled. They will unfold quickly.

47

59. 60.

Illus. 59. In ten minutes or so, the surface area of the wings has increased tenfold. This astonishing growth is due to a flow of blood which swells the veins, still soft as they are, and stretches them as far as they will go.

Here the wings are already smooth at the base. The edges are still crumpled.

Illus. 60. Hesitantly the butterfly takes its first steps and ventures along the branch.

61.

62.

Illus. 61. Now fully expanded, the wings are still limp and incapable of movement. The butterfly allows them to hang down, not touching each other. The air circulating around them will soon dry and harden them. The butterfly has now stopped growing and will not undergo any further changes, for it has at last become an adult or "perfect" insect.

Illus. 62. The butterfly practices coiling and uncoiling its proboscis.

A few hours after its hatching, the butterfly is dry. Its wings are now rigid; its muscles have achieved their full vigor. It looks for a clear space from which to launch itself, and climbs as high as it can.

Its movements are still clumsy. When it tries to take off, it falls into the grass. Patiently, it begins its climb again and reaches the tip of a yarrow (a small flowering herb) blooming in the sun. It rests on the flower, absorbing warmth (Illus. 63).

64. (magnified 3 times)

Every now and then the butterfly opens its wings wide and immediately brings them together again. It repeats the movement with increasing frequency and crawls about on the flower, trying to find the best direction in which to take off. It turns around and around with its antennae erect and its wings beating slowly and regularly.

Finally it remains still for a few seconds (Illus. 64), and suddenly, with no further trials, launches itself into space and flies. In a series of long glides with a few wing-beats in between, the butterfly is soon out of sight.

69.   (magnified 2.3 times)

The caterpillar had nibbled the rough leaves of the nettle with its pincer-like jaws. The butterfly feeds only on nectar given off by flowers, which it can reach and extract with its delicate, long and hollow proboscis (Illus. 69).

At rest, the proboscis is coiled up under the head, hidden between the two hairy palps (Illus. 65). When in quest of food, the butterfly uncoils it (66 and 67), inserts it deep into the petals and sucks up the nectar (68).

Sequence of 4 steps
65.-68.

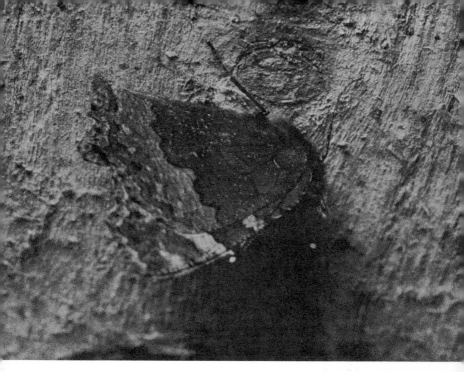

71. (magnified 2.5 times)

The Small Tortoise-Shells hatched in June live through the first weeks of summer and die before the autumn. The eggs which they lay in July produce a second brood of caterpillars, which pass through their cycle of transformations and develop into a second generation of butterflies.

Hatched in September, these butterflies feed on the flowers of late autumn (Illus. 70), and when the cold weather comes they seek a hiding place for the winter. The photograph above (Illus. 71) shows one of them hibernating under the roof of a barn. Not until spring will the survivors of this second generation mate. When they do, the cycle will begin again.

The life cycle of the Small Tortoise-Shell is pretty much the same as that of all butterflies. All pass through the same stages: egg, caterpillar, chrysalis, perfect butterfly. But to this general pattern Nature adds many marvelous variations.

The length of the entire cycle and of each phase varies according to the species. Some butterflies have only one generation in a year; others have two, three or more. Sometimes it is the adult which lives through the winter, hidden and asleep (Small Tortoise-Shell; Brimstone Butterfly). Sometimes the winter is passed in the egg state (as with the Silk Moth and Burnet) or in the chrysalis state of the life cycle (as the Swallowtail and Hawk Moth).

Each species of caterpillar behaves differently. The differences are particularly striking in the way the caterpillar changes to a chrysalis. Many caterpillars burrow into the ground; others remain in the open. Some hang from the tip of the abdomen like the Small Tortoise-Shell. Some, like the Swallowtail and the Whites, manufacture a silk thread which holds the chrysalis with its head upright. Others weave a protective cocoon.

The next pages show a few species whose development differs in some respect from that of the Small Tortoise-Shell.

These photographs have also been taken from life, in natural surroundings.

72.
Black-veined white
(magnified 2 times)

THE SWALLOWTAIL

The Small Tortoise-Shell lays its eggs on the nettle plant in April. The Swallowtail waits until July, when it lays its eggs, one by one, on the foliage of carrots or on some other plant of the carrot family (Illus. 73).

The young caterpillar (Illus. 74) is black, with patches of white on the middle of its body, which is covered with small spiky warts. It changes its coloring in each successive molt. When it reaches its maximum size its skin is smooth and green, and each ring is decorated with patches of black and orange dots. Illus. 75 shows the caterpillar hanging motionless on the stem of a seed-bearing plant, preparing to become a chrysalis.

74.
(magnified 10 times)

75.
(magnified 2 times)

3

76. (both photographs magnified 2.5 times) 77.

Unlike the Small Tortoise-Shell caterpillar, the Swallowtail caterpillar goes into the chrysalis state with its head upright. It too begins by weaving a silk pad on the stem, and attaches itself to the pad with the hooks on the legs at the end of its abdomen (Illus. 76). After it does this, it remains erect above its support.

The pictures show it manufacturing a silk cord and fastening both ends to the stem. It then thickens and strengthens the cord (77).

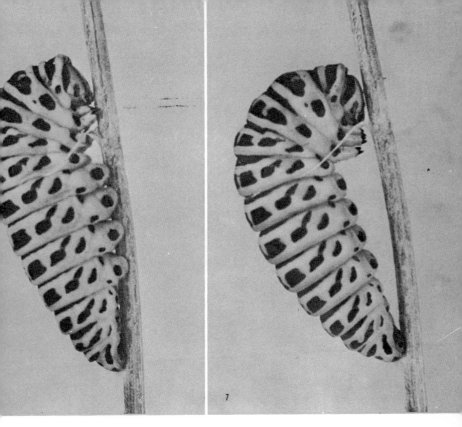

78.   (both photographs magnified 2.5 times)   79.

Illus. 78. When this task has been completed the caterpillar passes its head and body, as far as the fifth ring, through the loop of the cord.

Illus. 79. Only the two rear feet remain fastened to the pad; all the others lose their hold. But, caught by the looped girdle, the caterpillar does not fall. It remains fastened parallel to the stem.

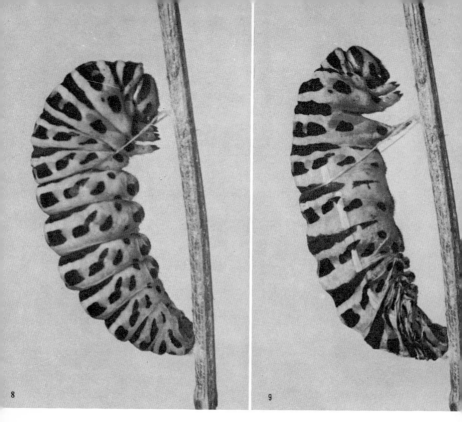

8   9

80.   (both photographs magnified 2.5 times)   81.

Illus. 80. After remaining motionless for 48 hours, the caterpillar comes to life again, pulls itself up, stretches, and swells out its body.

Illus. 81. This activity lasts for several hours, with short pauses for rest. At last the skin loosens, slips down and sags at the rear end.

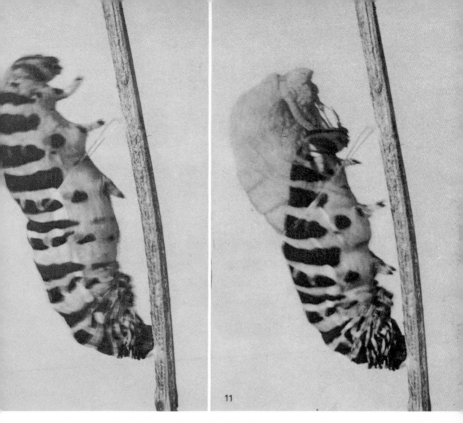

82.　　　(both photographs magnified 2.5 times)　　83.

Illus. 82. The skin splits behind the head; the swollen back of the chrysalis appears.

Illus. 83. The chrysalis gradually frees itself; it slips the cast-off skin skillfully under its girdle loop.

84.   (both photographs magnified 2.5 times)   85.

Illus. 84. The chrysalis is now almost clear of the skin. Only the end of the abdomen has to be freed.

Illus. 85. With the front part of its body firmly held between the girdle and the stem, it raises its abdomen, withdraws its cremaster and . . .

86. (both photographs magnified 2.5 times) 87.

Illus. 86. . . . fastens it directly to the silk pad. Its jerky movements have brought the girdle up to the third ring.

Illus. 87. As a result of these movements, the skin has become detached and has fallen clear of the chrysalis.

89.   (magnified 1.4 times)

Illus. 88. Within a few hours the chrysalis is in its final form. With its grayish-brown color it resembles a dead leaf or a broken piece of bark and can easily escape notice. This species spends the winter and spring in chrysalis form. The adult butterflies are found early in summer.

Illus. 89. The Swallowtail is the biggest and most brilliant European butterfly. Its yellow wings, with their curious "tails," are decorated with black bands sprinkled with blue dots. It is found throughout July in fields of clover and other herbs. It soars in flight, frequently flying high up among the flowers on a mountainside.

88.
(magnified 4 times)

Sequence of 5 steps

90.
(magnified 1.5 times)

THE SPURGE
HAWK MOTH

The large caterpillar of the Spurge Hawk moth is elegantly wrapped in a black skin with splashes of yellow and red. At its rear it bears a horn which looks menacing but is, in fact, soft and useless (Illus. 90).

91.   (magnified 2 times)

Instead of undergoing its metamorphosis in the open, like the Small Tortoise-Shell or the Swallowtail, the Spurge Hawk caterpillar finds an underground hiding place for its transformation. It slips under the moss or, with great difficulty, into the mold at the foot of a tree or a large stone. A little distance down it makes itself a small den, lines it with a scanty coating of silk, and changes into a large brown chrysalis veined with gray. Illus. 91 shows the den opened. The caterpillar's cast-off skin is next to the chrysalis. In this state the Spurge Hawk passes the autumn, winter and spring.

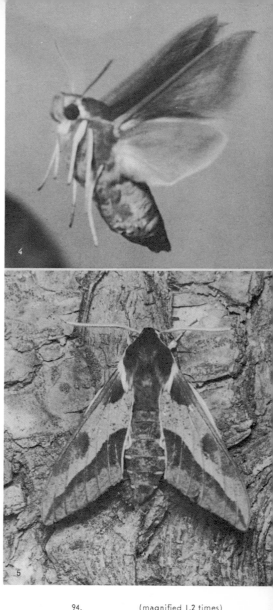

In June or July the moth leaves its chrysalis and makes its way out of its underground hiding place. It then climbs up to the first suitable resting place it finds. There it unfolds and strengthens its wings, which are still limp. The moth shown in Illus. 92 has reached this stage. It has not yet uncoiled its proboscis.

The Spurge Hawk moth becomes active only at night. It sips nectar while hovering in front of the flowers. Its flight is very rapid and its narrow pointed wings beat very quickly (Illus. 93). This photo was taken at 1/1000 of a second.

94.   (magnified 1.2 times)

During the day it sleeps on a tree trunk (Illus. 94), its green and gray coloring blending with the bark.

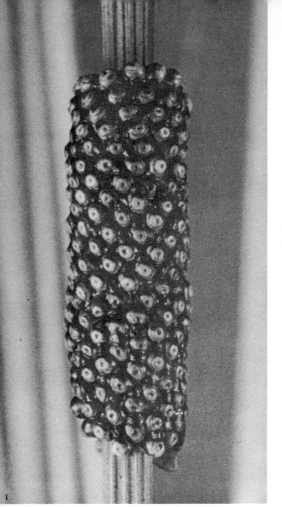

Sequence of 16 steps
95.
(magnified 10 times)

THE GROUND
LACKEY MOTH

Illus. 95. The Ground Lackey moth lays its eggs in the autumn. It arranges them regularly in a sleeve around a stalk of grass or a reed. When the gum covering them dries, the eggs stick firmly together. This is the state in which the eggs remain all through the winter.

96.   (magnified 2 times)

Illus. 96. Hatching in early summer, the caterpillars feed on many different plants. This photo shows caterpillars sunning themselves on alder leaves which they have carpeted with silk.

97.   (both photographs magnified 2 times)   98.

The caterpillars of Ground Lackey moths do not pupate (change into a chrysalis) in the open air. Nor do they bury themselves like those of the Spurge Hawk moth. They build a silk cocoon for a shelter.

Illus. 97. The caterpillar shown here has settled on some bilberry leaves. It covers the leaves with silk and stretches thicker strands from one leaf to another. Then it takes up its position in the center of the

99.   (both photographs magnified 2 times)   100.

structure and begins to wrap itself in a network of silk (Illus. 98).

Illus. 99 and 100. The caterpillar is now completely enclosed in its cocoon. It is barely visible as it continues to strengthen the protective wall from within. Altogether it spins several hundred yards of silk to form a closely woven outer coating.

101.   (magnified 2 times)

Illus. 101. This photograph, taken against the light, shows a caterpillar of the Ground Lackey moth completing its cocoon.

Within this silken retreat the caterpillar changes into a chrysalis. Illus. 102 and 103 show the same cocoon, first closed and then artificially opened.

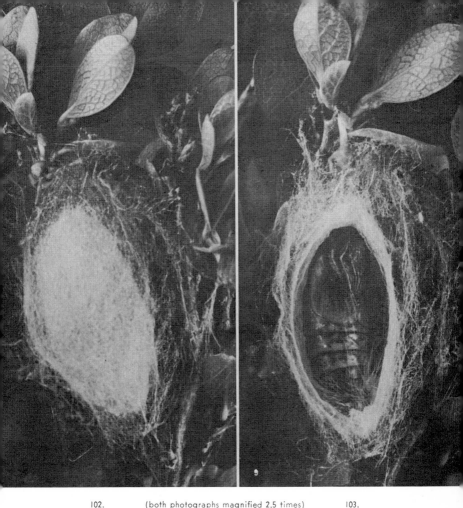

102.   (both photographs magnified 2.5 times)   103.

The wall of the cocoon is formed of two separate
layers. The chrysalis rests within. The caterpillar's skin
(its long hairs can be seen) has sunk down to the foot
of the cocoon. In a few weeks, at the beginning of
autumn, the moth will be ready to hatch.

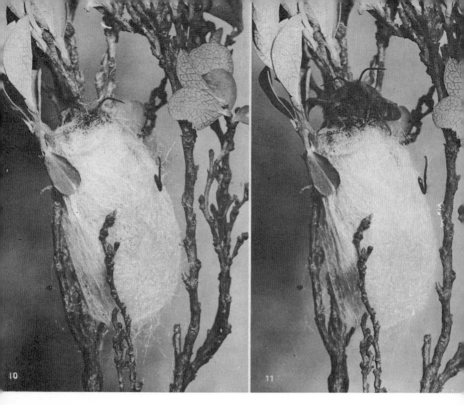

104.   (both photographs magnified 2 times)   105.

The moment of hatching has arrived.

To reach the open air, the moth must first come out of its chrysalis and then break through the wall of the cocoon.

Illus. 104. Pushing aside the tangle of threads with its head and legs, the moth tries to free itself. Its antennae already show.

106.   (both photographs magnified 2 times)   107.

Illus. 105. Slowly and with difficulty, the little brown moth pulls itself out through the narrow opening.

Illus. 106. Its broad abdomen makes the hole larger as it passes through. Its wings, limp and crumpled, are still very small.

Illus. 107. Free at last, the moth hangs from a branch, resting after the double labor of hatching and breaking out of the cocoon.

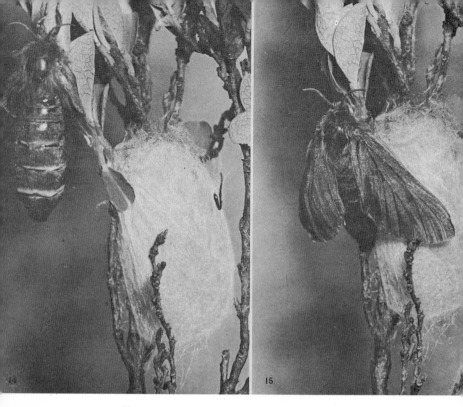

Illus. 108. We can tell that this moth is a female from the enormous heavy abdomen, swollen with eggs, and the thin antennae.

Illus. 109. Gradually the wings expand. This moth, however, will not make much use of them, because the female hardly flies at all and does not even feed herself. Once hatched, she waits for the male Ground Lackey moth who will fertilize her eggs.

Illus. 110. The male — just emerged from an identical cocoon — is smaller and more active. He has enormous feathery antennae, and his brown wings are decorated with two yellow bands.

110.

The Ground Lackey moths have a very short span of life. They are born, mate, lay their eggs, and die — all within a period of a few days.

112. (magnified 4 times)

THE HYLOPHILA

The attractive caterpillar of the HYLOPHILA (Illus. 111) lives on beeches and oaks in forests. Its smooth skin is delicate green, sprinkled with yellow dots and lines. Its rear legs, spread and curved under at the ends, enable it to cling securely to the bark of twigs and branches.

The caterpillar spins its cocoon on the flat surface of a beech leaf (Illus. 112). The work is completed within a few hours. In autumn the leaf falls from the tree, and the cocoon passes the winter on the ground.

Sequence of 5 steps

111.
(magnified 4 times)

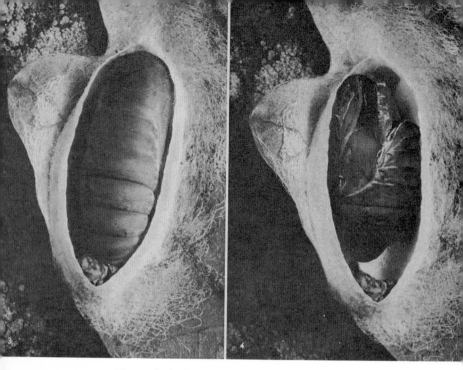

113.　(both photographs magnified 3 times)　114.

A cocoon has been opened to show the chrysalis (Illus. 113). In front of the chrysalis, toward the top, there is an opening in the cocoon. The edges are held together by the elasticity of the silk. The moth then only needs to push with its head to get out. Behind the chrysalis, the caterpillar's cast-off skin has settled down at the foot of the cocoon.

Illus. 114 shows the empty and damaged chrysalis after hatching. The opening in the cocoon closes up after the moth comes out.

Illus. 115. The Hylophila is an attractive moth with a wing span just under 1¼ inches.

115.   (magnified 7 times)

Sequence of 5 steps.   117.   (both photographs magnified 2.5 times)   118.

THE BURNET

Illus. 117. The caterpillar of the BURNET moth is yellow with black spots. Here it prepares to weave its cocoon on a stalk of grass.

Illus. 118. The cocoon is fastened to the stalk by a delicate sheath of silk in the shape of a spindle. It is closely woven and shimmering, with a paper-like finish. The photograph on the opposite page (116) shows several of these cocoons.

119.   (both photographs magnified 2.5 times)   120.

The cocoon has been opened to show the black chrysalis of the Burnet (Illus. 119).

The rings are flexible at the joints, so that the insect can wriggle about very nimbly. Before it hatches, it can raise itself to the top of the cocoon or even burst through it. Then in one final effort it rips the skin of the chrysalis and comes out into the air. Illus. 120

121.   (magnified 2.5 times)

shows the empty shell of the chrysalis stuck in the top
of the cocoon.

Illus. 121. The Burnets are small, clumsy and lazy.
They sip the nectar of primroses, clover, and thistles.
Their mating takes place on grasses. While their
activities take place during the day, they belong
structurally to the moths rather than to the butterflies.

The butterflies and moths whose life history we have studied are just a very small sample of the hundred thousand or so species known throughout the world. They range in infinite variety from the great Geometer of Brazil, with its wing span of nearly 13 inches, to a tiny clothes moth with a span of only about 1/10 of an inch.

Of the many moths, a few are large and handsome, but most are of modest size and coloring. Among the butterflies, we find the simplest shapes and patterns and the most fantastic. Many have gaudy colors and others are the dowdiest of grays and browns. Fascinating as they are, the perfect insects are often equalled or even surpassed in beauty and strangeness by the caterpillars, and sometimes by the chrysalises. It is not, however, always true that an attractive caterpillar produces an attractive butterfly or moth.

122.
Scarce Copper
(magnified 8 times)

INDEX

93

legs
  Fritillary, 9
  Ground Lackey Moth, 78
  Small Tortoise-Shell, 24, 34, 39
life span, 5, 53
mating
  Burnet, 89
  Small Tortoise-Shell, 15, 16
metamorphosis, 34
moult, 22
  Small Tortoise-Shell, 24–31, 43
  Swallowtail, 59
moths, 10, 11
nectar, 13, 53, 71, 89
nettle, 16–18, 20, 30, 31, 33, 43, 53, 58
Nun Moth, 10, 11
palps *see* feelers
proboscis, 46
  Small Tortoise-Shell, 46, 49, 53
  Spurge Hawk Moth, 71
pupate, 74
rings, caterpillar
  Burnet, 88
  Small Tortoise-Shell, 34
  Swallowtail, 58, 61
saliva, 20
Scarce Copper, 91
silk, 20, 22, 24, 26, 30, 31, 34, 38–40,
    60, 61, 65, 69, 87

Silk Moth, 57
skin
  Burnet, 88
  Ground Lackey Moth, 69
  Hylophila, 83, 84
  Small Tortoise-Shell, 22, 24–26, 29,
      36–41
  Spurge Hawk Moth, 69
  Swallowtail, 62, 63
Small Tortoise-Shell, 13–57
spines, 36, 37
Spurge Hawk Moth, 68–71
stigmata, 34
sunning, 15, 20, 31, 33
Swallowtail, 57–67
warts, 58
Whites, 57
wings, 13, 39
  Chalk-Hill Blue, 6
  Fritillary, 9
  Ground Lackey Moth, 79, 80
  Nun Moth, 11
  Pearl-Bordered Fritillary, 7
  Small Tortoise-Shell, 15, 16, 46–51
  Spurge Hawk Moth, 71
yarrow, 50